Dealing with Racism

Pete Sanders and Steve Myers

Aladdin / Watts
London • Sydney

© Aladdin Books Ltd 2004

Designed and produced by
Aladdin Books Ltd
28 Percy Street
London W1T 2BZ

New edition
first published in
Great Britain in 2004 by
Franklin Watts
96 Leonard Street
London EC2A 4XD

ISBN 0 7496 5492 9

Original edition published as
What Do You Know About –
Racism

A catalogue record for this
book is available from the
British Library.

Printed in UAE
Editor
Harriet Brown

Designers
Flick, Book Design & Graphics
Simon Morse

Illustrator
Mike Lacey

Picture Research
Brian Hunter Smart

CONTENTS

How to use this book

The books in this series deal with issues that affect the lives of many young people.

- Each book can be read by a young person alone, or together with an adult.

- Issues raised in the storyline are further discussed in accompanying text.

- Practical ideas are given in the 'What can we do?' section at the end of the book.

- Organisations and helplines are listed for additional information and support.

INTRODUCTION

> Today, most of us live in a mixed-race society, which represents a range of different people, cultures and beliefs.

The variety of different cultures can enrich our lives. Unfortunately, it also means that most of us will come into contact with racism and prejudice.

This book will help you to find out more about racism, the different ways in which people are racist and the reasons for their behaviour. Each chapter introduces a different aspect of the subject, illustrated by a continuing storyline. The characters in the story have to deal with situations which many of you may experience yourselves.

After each episode, we stop and look at the issues raised, and broaden the discussion. By the end, you should know more about racism, how it affects peoples lives and what can be done to challenge it.

WHAT IS RACISM?

> " There are over five billion people in the world, living in over 200 countries. We belong to different races, cultures and religions. "

Many people believe that these differences are there to be shared and celebrated. Some people, however, use them as an excuse to treat certain people as inferior in some way.

Racism exists in all races and cultures. It is more than just believing your own race is better than someone else's.

It is treating people differently and unfairly simply because they belong to a different race. Racists usually target those who are in the minority in society, but not always. In South Africa, a relatively small white population ruled the black majority for hundreds of years. Racism is anything said or done to harm, ridicule or disadvantage someone because of their race.

Racists choose not to see people as individuals, but as members of a group against which they are prejudiced.

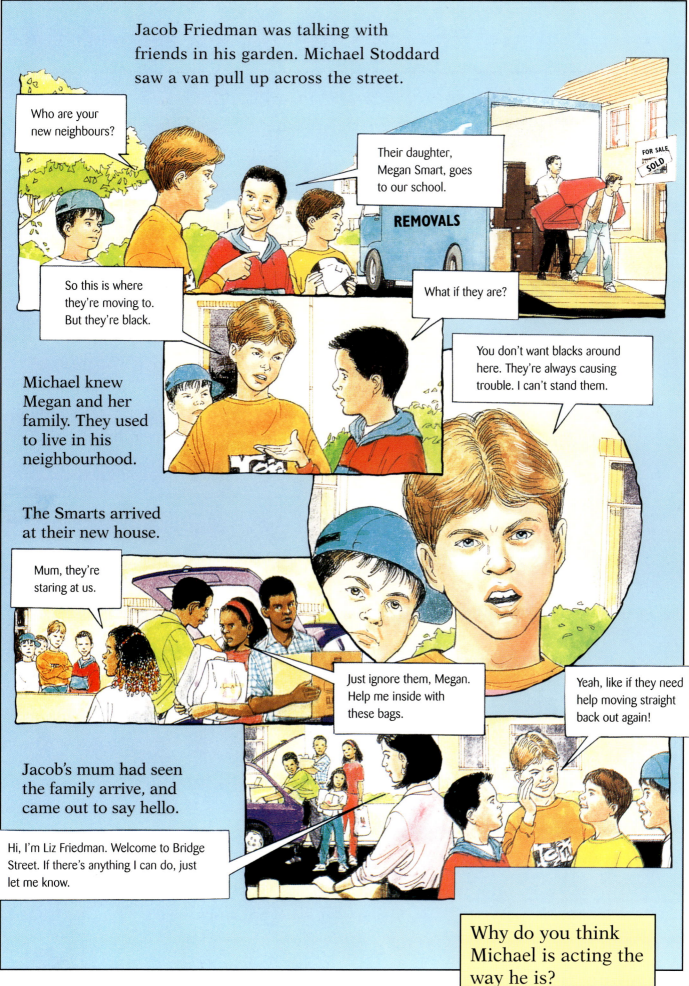

Jacob Friedman was talking with friends in his garden. Michael Stoddard saw a van pull up across the street.

Michael knew Megan and her family. They used to live in his neighbourhood.

The Smarts arrived at their new house.

Jacob's mum had seen the family arrive, and came out to say hello.

Why do you think Michael is acting the way he is?

5

Most racist beliefs are not founded on fact.

Michael is repeating comments he has heard, which are based on mistrust or hatred, not on evidence. He knows little about the Smart family personally. He is prejudiced against all black people because of lies and half-truths he has been told by others. Information that purposely misleads people into believing something which may not be true is called 'propaganda'. Michael has been listening to racist propaganda.

You don't want blacks around here. They're always causing trouble.

Michael is stereotyping black people.

He is using generalisations to apply to a whole group of people. This is like saying that all boys like to play football, or all girls play with dolls. Comments such as these may be true for some people, but they do not apply to everyone. This kind of stereotyping helps racists, because it refuses to see people as individuals. Racist stereotypes are usually very negative and can have damaging effects on individuals and on society as a whole.

By jumping to conclusions, you may miss out on what other people have to offer.

You don't have to like everybody – each person has strengths and weaknesses. Being non-racist does not mean that you cannot dislike or disagree with someone of a different race from your own. But your judgement should be based on what you find out about each particular person. It is never helpful to pre-judge anybody. This only creates barriers between you and others, before you even get to know them.

6

DIFFERENT KINDS OF RACISM

" The most obvious type of racism occurs when people are singled out because of the colour of their skin. But this is not the only kind. **"**

Racists may also pick on people because they come from a different country or culture, or belong to a different religion.

Racism takes many different forms. You may have seen racists calling people rude names, or making fun of the way they dress, or the food they eat. Sometimes racists try to make others feel small or unwanted. They might prevent someone from taking part in an activity, and try to make others do the same. More and more racist attacks involve violence, and these can often be very serious indeed.

Racism is not always obvious. Sometimes, plausible excuses are given to disguise a racist action. For instance, white parents may move their child from a mixed-race school, saying the new school will offer the child a better education. It could be that the real reason might be that they do not want their child mixing with children from other cultures.

Some racist acts may seem minor compared to others, but this does not make them any more acceptable. All kinds of racism are wrong and unacceptable.

Some people make no attempt to mix with others from different cultures. They might ignore them completely, treating them as if they didn't exist.

7

8

If it isn't blackie and paki. Are these two bothering you, Jacob?

Michael knows that he can hurt the girls' feelings by calling them names.
Racists like to label people as another way of denying their individuality. These words may sound very mild, but they can still be deeply hurtful. It is important to use language carefully, and be aware of the effect your words may have. Avoid using words to label people. The way you express your ideas will show respect or disrespect for other people's cultures.

Children from mixed-race families sometimes face problems.

- Some children have one black parent and one white one.

- This may make them the targets of racism from both black people and white people.

James was not pleased to see Megan with Jacob.
When people from different ethnic backgrounds become friends, their families and others close to them may have strong views about the situation. They may not want their relationship to continue. This is a form of prejudice. There can be religious or cultural differences to cope with, but these need not be a barrier. Many people enjoy successful mixed-race relationships.

They said I didn't have enough experience. But I know it's because I'm black.

James feels he didn't get the job because he is black.
Racial discrimination is when someone is disadvantaged because of their race, culture or religion. It is against the law in many countries to discriminate like this. The colour of a person's skin has nothing to do with their ability to do a job. Unfortunately, many organisations find ways around the law.

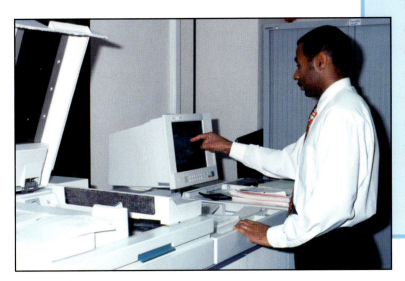

WHY ARE PEOPLE RACIST?

> Racism is often based on ignorance and fear of anything unfamiliar. Instead of finding out about other cultures, racists choose to hate or despise anyone who is different.

People are not born racist. Their views develop as they grow up. Some young people live in a situation where family or friends are racist. They may believe that racism is normal and acceptable and adopt the same ideas themselves.

Racists may see other cultures as a threat to their own. Many claim to be acting for the good of their country, to keep their own race 'pure' – separate and distinct from others. They view anyone of a different race, even those born in the same country, as an outsider. Sticking together and sharing ideas with people who think in the same way reinforces this kind of prejudice.

Some racism is caused by a desire to gain or maintain advantage over others. If one section of a community has an advantage over another section, members of the advantaged group may wish to hold on to their privilege or power. They may not want the situation to become more equal.

In some places in the past, black and white people were kept separate on buses and trains, in cinemas, and even on park benches.

11

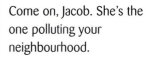

Come on, Jacob. She's the one polluting your neighbourhood.

It can be great fun to spend time with friends.

Gangs like Michael's, though, can cause trouble. It is easy in a gang situation to be swept along by what the gang's doing, even if you don't want to take part. It can be hard to speak out against the group. Racists often use this to their advantage. Some racist attacks are carried out by mobs of people. In the heat of an argument, some people may not realise what they are doing, or may go further than they intended.

People often have very strong views about the area they live in.

Mr Stoddard's remarks are based on the idea that different cultures should not mix with one another. In some countries this has even led to a separation of different groups of people. Under the system of 'apartheid', black South Africans were not allowed to live in the same town, use the same public transportation or the same beach as white people. When a group of people is confined to one area in this way, the neighbourhood is called a 'ghetto'.

What's up – do you like her or something?

Jacob could have spoken up for Megan, but he chose to stay silent.

Racists often rely on people being afraid to challenge them. If those around them refused to accept their behaviour, they might think twice about continuing. Ignoring racism only helps it to develop. If you don't speak out against racism you will appear to be going along with it.

13

THE EFFECTS OF RACISM

" Racism is something that affects everybody. Racists miss the opportunity to learn about other cultures and about people as individuals. "

Those who are being victimised by racists may become racist themselves, as a way of dealing with what is happening.

If you are being picked on by racists, you might become lonely and depressed. You might try to avoid situations where racism could occur, and pretend to be sick, or play truant from school. If you are experiencing threats or violence, you might become scared to leave the safety of home. The worry could make it difficult to sleep properly, and your work might suffer. Sometimes people who are experiencing racism start to accept it as a way of life, and expect racist incidents to continue. They might even think that they are in some way to blame for the situation. If you are always being told that you are inferior, you may eventually start to believe that this is so. Sometimes, racism leads to violence. It may result in fights between individuals or 'rival' gangs, or even worse, in war. Racism has caused wars all over the world.

Racist views have been the cause of wars, both between different countries and between groups of people in the same country.

It was 8.15...

... and Megan still had not come down for breakfast.

Megan, you're going to be late for school.

Megan, what are you doing? Why aren't you dressed?

There was no reply. Mrs Smart went upstairs to Megan's room.

Suddenly Megan began to cry. She told her mum about the racist bullies.

You promised things would be different here.

Mrs Smart told Megan she couldn't help if she didn't know who was responsible.

Is it Jacob? I've seen him playing with Michael Stoddard. The Stoddards like causing trouble.

We hoped they would be. Who is it who's saying things?

I can't tell you, Mum. I'm afraid.

She's beginning to think it's her own fault. What are we going to do?

That evening...

First James and now Megan. It's so unfair.

I know. It looks like moving hasn't solved anything.

I don't know, but we're not going to put up with it anymore.

The Smarts had decided to move after James had been beaten up on his way home.

What do you think the Smarts should do?

15

The way we feel about ourselves is influenced by the way others treat us. Many racists are aware of this. Like Michael, they use racism to frighten and ridicule people, even to the point where they begin to doubt their own self worth. Racists might deny you the right to succeed, by making you believe you don't deserve success. Or they may make you think that you are not good at something. This can lower your expectations of yourself and may prevent you from achieving as much as you could have otherwise.

> It looks like moving hasn't solved anything. But we're not going to put up with it anymore.

The Smart family hoped that a move to a new house would help escape racists. A problem can sometimes become so bad that it seems running away from it is the only answer. But it is not always possible to escape racism in this way. Sometimes, situations have to be faced up to, however difficult that may be.

Michael and his gang are bullies.

Racism is a form of bullying, and bullying is always wrong.

● Racists may say that it is 'just a bit of fun'. But racism is very serious and it can have a huge effect on your self-esteem.

● Nobody should have to put up with bullying or racism.

● It is essential to remember that you are in the right, and it is the racists who are at fault.

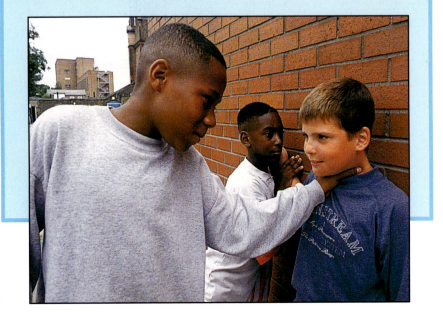

HIDDEN RACISM

" Some people find ways to cover up racist actions. Others, however, may not even realise that they are being racist. **"**

Hidden racism is difficult to challenge, because no one seems to be purposely acting in a racist way, and no one appears to be directly affected. But hidden racism can be just as damaging as open racism.

Hidden racism helps to develop ideas that are stereotyped and inaccurate. The way races are shown in books and on TV is often incorrect. In 'Wild West' films, 'Indians' – Native Americans – are usually shown as savages. In reality, many tribes were non-violent, and only fought to protect their land. A news item on TV or in a newspaper may mention a person's colour in connection with a story, even though it is completely irrelevant. If the story happens to concern a crime, this can set up a negative idea in the mind of the person reading or watching. People in countries where there is famine are presented as helpless and in need of our pity. These images can take away people's dignity and encourage us to believe all those in developing countries need help.

Hidden racism is dangerous. It is important never to take for granted what you see or hear. You should only judge a situation once you have a full picture of it.

Races are often shown in an inaccurate way on TV and in books. It is important not to judge people or situations until you know the full story.

Without telling Megan, the Smarts went to see the headteacher, Mr Samuels.

This is very serious. We don't tolerate racism at this school.

We have strict rules to make sure everyone is treated equally. Any reports of racism are dealt with severely.

Mr Samuels told the Smarts what the school did to stop racism.

Mr Samuels promised he would try to sort out the issue.

There are many different cultures within the school. We try to celebrate them all.

It all sounds very nice. But we still have a problem.

The next day...

... Jane Smart met Liz Friedman.

How are you settling in?

Jane told Liz about the racism and that she thought Jacob might be involved.

Ok, except for some problems Megan's having at school.

I'm sure you're wrong. Jacob wouldn't do anything like that.

Jacob knows I won't stand for racism. We're Jewish, Mrs Smart – we've had our share of racist comments.

I think he's being influenced by Michael Stoddard.

It's different for you. You're still white.

What do you think Mrs Smart means?

18

We have strict rules to make sure everyone is treated equally. Reports of racism are dealt with severely.

Many organisations today have equal opportunities policies.

These are meant to make sure that nobody is discriminated against because of their colour, gender, disability, class, religious beliefs, age or sexuality. Just having the policy may not always be enough to prevent discrimination. To stop racism, everybody must be aware of the policy and agree to stick to its rules. There must also be strict procedures to deal with anyone who breaks these rules.

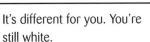

It's different for you. You're still white.

Most racists target anyone whom they see as different.

As Mrs Smart has pointed out, however, some differences are more obvious than others. For instance, a racist may not be able to tell if you are Jewish simply by looking at you. Fear of racial abuse may make some people try to hide or deny their race or religion. This is another kind of hidden racism. Your own culture is something you should be able to be proud of.

Making sure all cultures are positively represented in society is essential in challenging racism.

However, it is important that it is a true representation. You may have seen movies where there is one 'token' black character among a large number of white ones. Tokenism is not effective in challenging racism, and may even add to it.

THE HISTORY OF RACISM

> Throughout history, billions of people have suffered and died as a result of prejudice and hatred.

Millions of Jews, Poles, Gypsies and Soviets were imprisoned in concentration camps and killed during the Second World War.

Racism has affected people both as individuals and as groups. Most examples of racism involving individuals have gone unrecorded – they were never reported or written down.

Over the last 500 years, much racism has been a result of the colonies established by white Europeans in Africa, Asia, North and South America, and Australia. European settlers claimed the land and resources of these countries for themselves and their own nations. History books often talk about the discovery of new lands, as though they did not exist before they were visited by white explorers. The native inhabitants had their rights and lands taken from them. Europeans even enslaved millions of Africans and sold them as servants and cheap labour for the plantations. Slavery was not abolished in England and the United States until the 19th century.

The 20th century also saw great cruelty and suffering caused by racism. During the 1930s and 1940s, Nazi Germany persecuted Jewish people across Europe and sent millions of Jews to concentration camps. Six million Jews were murdered by the Nazis. Even until the early 1990s, black South Africans were ruled under the apartheid system by white people descended from European settlers.

That evening...

... Jacob's mum confronted him.

It was Michael, really. I just happened to be there.

And said nothing. That's as bad as joining in.

I didn't mean any harm.

You of all people should know how dangerous racism is.

When they were his age, Jacob's grandparents had had to leave Austria when the Nazis took over.

Jacob had heard about this before, but was just beginning to understand fully.

They were lucky. Millions of Jews were killed. If ordinary Germans had done something to try and stop the Nazis, many of those people might not have died.

It wasn't easy once they got to this country, either. They were treated as second-class citizens. People were very racist.

Jacob realised the devastating effect racism can have on people's lives.

I'll apologise to Megan. I should have done something.

> You of all people should know how dangerous racism is.

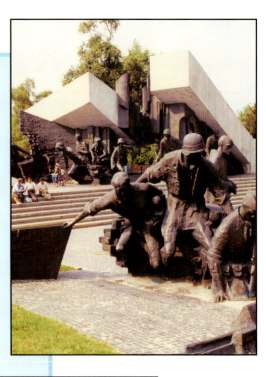

Although Jacob had heard about the events of the Second World War before, he is beginning to realise the true horror of what happened. The Nazis blamed Jewish people for the problems of their society. Jews were thrown out of their homes. Many Jews were sent to concentration camps, where millions died. However, there are still groups of racists today who try to deny that these events, known as the holocaust, ever happened. This is yet another example of racism.

> It wasn't easy when they got to this country, either. They were treated as second-class citizens.

Jacob now knows that no-one must forget the terrible consequences of racism. At the same time, it is not helpful to go on blaming new generations of people for the actions of their parents or grandparents. You cannot change what has happened in the past. Racism relies on people continuing to be prejudiced against one another. It can only be stopped by putting aside grudges and resentments and talking openly.

Jacob's grandparents escaped the Nazis, but met a different kind of prejudice when they came to the UK. Like other groups of people moving to new countries, they had no choice but to accept the poorly-paid work that nobody else wanted to do. In the past, some countries have even encouraged people to leave their homeland for this reason. When jobs became hard to find, the immigrants were resented for having work, while those born in the country had none.

RACISM TODAY

> Studying history can help us to learn from the mistakes others have made in the past. Unfortunately, this does not always prevent us from repeating them.

In some countries today, the situation has improved for those who were the target of racism and prejudice. However, this has often happened too slowly, and not always effectively.

In many countries, minority groups now have full rights as citizens, and racism is illegal. But laws do not necessarily change people's attitudes, and racist acts continue to happen. There have been some dramatic changes. Apartheid has now been abolished in South Africa, and black people have the right to vote for the government. But in many countries, racism continues to cause war and suffering. Following the break-up of Yugoslavia, for example, thousands have been killed in racial conflict, and millions more are refugees. In Rwanda, in East Africa, one million people died in a racial fight for power. In Zimbabwe, there are government-led attacks on the white minority. Today, racism is more widely recognised than in the past, but it is still a major problem which affects the whole of society.

International agencies such as the UN (United Nations) are sometimes needed to help a country that has been torn apart by a racially-motivated war.

Mr Samuels told the class that a parent had complained of racism.

So what? I wouldn't blame them.

I'll bet it was that Megan's mum and dad.

Aida's just joined the school. She's from Iraq, and doesn't speak our language yet.

In class, the teacher introduced a new girl.

She must be thick if she doesn't speak English.

Mayumi didn't speak English two years ago, and she's much cleverer than you.

I'll bet her parents don't have jobs. You know who will end up paying for them.

Us, as usual.

That's a horrible thing to say, Michael.

The teacher heard what Michael had said.

My dad says we have enough problems in this country. People shouldn't be allowed in so easily.

Your dad doesn't know what he's talking about. It's not easy. There are loads of rules.

The teacher tried to explain the situation, but Michael refused to listen.

Try to imagine yourself in Aida's position, Michael.

How do you think Aida feels?

24

Aida's just joined the school. She's from Iraq and doesn't speak our language yet.

Aida is a refugee, forced to seek shelter in a new country.
Like many of the millions of refugees in the world today, she has been forced to flee because of violence and racism. Refugees often leave their homes at short notice because their lives are in danger. Most are forced to abandon everything. Reaching a new country, they may be shocked and scared because of the dangers and hardships they have experienced.

Ethnic cleansing has been responsible for the deaths of thousands of people.
'Ethnic cleansing' is the term used to describe killing people of a different race or culture and taking over their land. The idea is to ensure that all the people who live in a certain area are of the same race or religion. It is based on the false belief that one race is purer than another.

My dad says we have enough problems in this country. People shouldn't be allowed in so easily.

Michael's father believes that all immigrants are a burden to society. This is not true.
The immigration laws in most countries are very strict. Refugees are not allowed in without a good reason. Some do arrive in their new country with nothing because they have had to leave everything behind. Others have family or jobs to go to. All must try to begin a new life in a strange country, and need support and understanding. Being in a new place is often very hard to adjust to. Racism can make the change even more difficult.

Language differences

- If you were taken to a foreign country, and were unable to communicate, this would not mean that you were any less intelligent.

- Some people do not believe that they should have to know another language. Yet they expect others to be able to speak theirs!

CHALLENGING RACISM

"There is no easy answer to the problem of racism. The first step in stopping it is to understand that it exists and to recognise when it is happening."

Racism is always unacceptable. Some racist acts are more severe than others, but all racism should be challenged.

The way this can be done will vary depending on the situation. You will need to judge when it is best to leave a situation quietly, and when to stand up for yourself. Sometimes it is possible to challenge racism personally. At other times it may be better to involve other people.

In many schools, young people and adults work together to produce anti-racist policies. Working with others in a group can help to improve things. Adults may urge politicians to press for anti-racist laws, and support political candidates who share their views.

Many companies, when advertising for jobs, try to attract applications from ethnic minorities. In many countries, the government recognises racism as being wrong, and has made laws to protect people's rights. Some people believe these laws need to be enforced more strongly.

Racism has a negative effect on everyone's life. By opposing it at every opportunity, we can show that we value all members of society.

One way of challenging racism is to organise peaceful marches to protest against discrimination. Violent protests are not a good way of getting a message across.

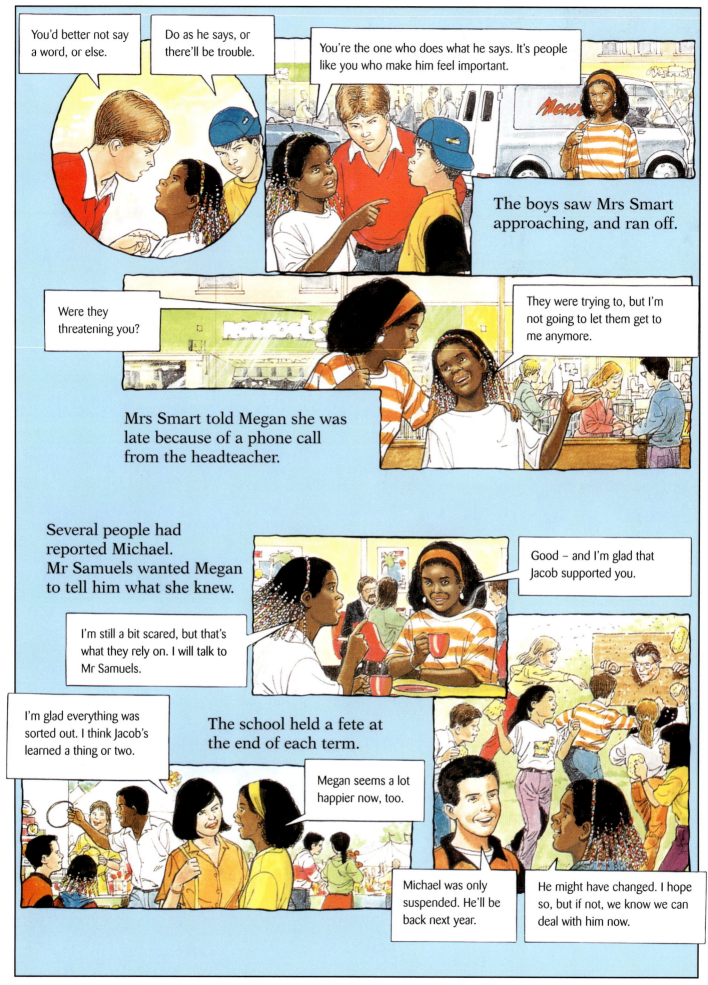

There are no enemies, just ignorant people like you and your dad.

It is important not to judge people by what others tell you.
As Jacob has learned, you need to make up your own mind, and not be influenced by other people's opinions. It takes time to get to know someone. Making assumptions and jumping to conclusions about people will not help. Ignorance only gets in the way of a possible friendship or relationship.

All you know how to do is hit people.

Many racist attacks have involved violence. But as Jacob knows, reacting to violence with more violence will solve nothing.
Often a violent response makes a situation worse. It is more effective to challenge racism by discussing differences and similarities between people. Discussion can often show that we have many things in common. And instead of being afraid of our differences, we can share and enjoy them.

Ignoring racism will not make it go away.
In the end, Megan and Jacob had to confront the racists.

- If racist bullies are allowed to get away with their behaviour, they will continue to harass others. If they are not challenged, their confidence may grow.

29

WHAT CAN WE DO?

> Having read this book, you will understand more about how racism affects everyone's lives.

You will know that you should never ignore racism, and how important it is to consider the best way of handling it effectively.

Judge each situation carefully. If you are personally being subjected to racist abuse, you will need to decide whether you can deal with the situation alone, or whether you should involve others to help you to challenge it. Racists need help too, particularly in recognising their racism and understanding that it is unacceptable. If you have ever been racist, it might be worthwhile to think about why you acted the way you did.

It may help to think about the effect your action had on the other person's well-being. Most of us have absorbed racist messages at some point in our lives. Knowing this enables us to challenge our own ideas and behaviour. This is important, even if we believe ourselves to be non-racist.

Adults can help too, by understanding how their words and actions can influence young people. Young people often copy what adults do, and the words they use. If adults around them are racist, they may start to be racist too.

Adults and young people who have read this book together may find it helpful to share their ideas. Anyone who is experiencing problems with racism, or would like to know more, can contact the organisations listed below.

Anti Nazi League
(The ANL aim to stop the Nazis reaching a wider audience and growing.)
PO Box 2566
London
N4 1WJ
Tel: +44 (0) 20 7924 0333
Email:
enquiries@anl.org.uk
Website: www.anl.org.uk

Campaign Against Racism and Fascism
BM Box 8784
London
WC1N 3XX,
Tel: +44 (0) 20 7837 1450
Email:
info@carf.demon.co.uk
Website:
www.carf.demon.co.uk

Commission for Racial Equality
(Tackles racial discrimination and promotes racial equality.)
Head Office
St Dunstan's House
201-211 Borough High St
London
SE1 1GZ
Tel: +44 (0) 20 7939 0000
Email: info@cre.gov.uk
Website: www.cre.gov.uk

Institute for Race Relations
(IRR campaign for racial justice)
2-6 Leeke Street
London
WC1X 9HS
Tel: +44 (0) 20 7837 0041
Email: info@irr.org.uk
Website: www.irr.org.uk

Kick It Out
(Working throughout the football, educational and community sectors to challenge racism.)
PO Box 29544
London
EC2A 4WR
Tel: +44 (0) 20 7684 4884
Email: info@kickitout.org
Website: www.kickitout.org

Minority Rights Group International
(Promoting co-operation and understanding)
54 Commercial Street
London
E1 6LT
Tel: +44 (0) 20 7422 4200
E-mail:
minority.rights@mrgmail.org
Website:
www.minorityrights.org

National Assembly Against Racism (NAAR)
28 Commercial Street
London
E1 6LS
Tel: +44 (0) 20 7247 9907
Email: info@naar.org.uk
Website: www.naar.org.uk

The Monitoring Group
(Support and assistance for victims of racial harrassment.)
Emergency Helpline:
+44 (0) 800 374 618

Kidshelpline Australia
(A free 24-hour helpline for children.)
Tel: 1 800 551800

Racism. No Way!
(Assisting school communities to recognise and address racism in the learning environment.)
PO Box 590
Darlinghurst
NSW 2010
Australia
Email: webkeeper@ racismnoway.com.au
Website:
www.racismnoway.com.au

INDEX